Tuesday's Story

Becky Hohnstein

Copyright © 2021 by Becky Hohnstein. 834077

All rights reserved. No part of this book may be reproduced or transmitted in any form or by any means, electronic or mechanical, including photocopying, recording, or by any information storage and retrieval system, without permission in writing from the copyright owner.

To order additional copies of this book, contact:
Xlibris
844-714-8691
www.Xlibris.com
Orders@Xlibris.com

ISBN: Softcover   978-1-6641-9439-7
Hardcover   978-1-6641-9442-7
EBook   978-1-6641-9440-3

Print information available on the last page

Rev. date: 11/09/2021

Dedicated to

Emmit, Bogey`s best friend.

Introduction

Tuesday was born on a Wednesday, after a few weeks, she came to us on a Saturday. She was named on a Monday and left me on a Friday.

This is *Tuesday's* story.

We who choose to surround ourselves with lives even more temporary than our own live within a fragile circle, easily and often breached. Unable to accept its awful gaps, we still would live no other way. We cherish memory as the only certain immortality, never fully understanding the necessary plan.

SEPARATE LIFETIMES
"The Once Again Prince"
by Irving Townsend

Tuesday was a gift to my husband and me,
a furry, white bundle under the Christmas tree.

A spirited puppy, much play she commanded when tired she slept wherever she landed.

Tracking in the snow, her nose such a sight would turn from black to winter white.

One day she ran too far and too fast,
from the cold she was snatched up, at last.

Tuesday was growing from puppy to dog,
it happened so quickly we were all agog.

With black nose
   and eyes
and often black paws,
   she became
a frisky cocker
   with a mighty cause.

She dug in the mud, her curly spattered locks,
once clean and white, now a grubby mask and socks.

A bathtub grapple
and some time,
we found our Tuesday
with much less grime.

Running in the sand, enjoying the sun, getting muddy again was a lot of fun.

But all by herself
the fun came to an end,
until she spotted
a spotted friend.

As Tuesday got older, things she liked lots, was hanging around cats and flower pots.

Tuesday had a black and white friend.
Checkers was her bud
on which she would depend.

Checker`s game was to hide, but cobwebs told all, he`d been under a chair in the basement hall.

One day he woke Tuesday with a plan quick and neat.
The goal was for a spooky Halloween trick-or-treat.

Tuesday was all ready,
 her devil outfit on tight,
when we knew checkers would be
 a more devilish sight.

So Tuesday, as a devil, was not meant to be, and soon she was dressed as a sweet bumblebee.

Checkers, the silly…

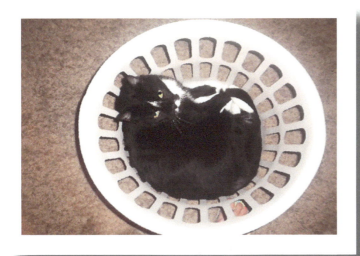

basket cat…

pillow cat…

drawer cat and…

box cat.

Tuesday had another cat friend, Susie, and she was quite a little doozy.

Susie and Tuesday were spunky, fun gals,
they hung out together and were great pals.

Susie the silly…

cable box cat…

flower cat…

TV cat and…

sack cat.

Our warm season ended,
   it snowed all day.
Tuesday wanted out
   so she could go play.

When she could take the cold no more,
a path she forged to the front door.

Once inside, dried off in my lap,
then under the covers
for a snuggly nap.

As Christmas, soon,
    was drawing near,
I dressed Tuesday all up
    in reindeer gear.

She finally dropped that bah humbug sneer, and became a whimsical and happy reindeer.

Christmas was over and the snow came back.
Drifts in our yard, we did not lack.

Tuesday was outside, but where could she be?
The design on the step said she`d been there recently.

The paw prints, oh good, another clue
Tuesday`s time to come in was overdue.

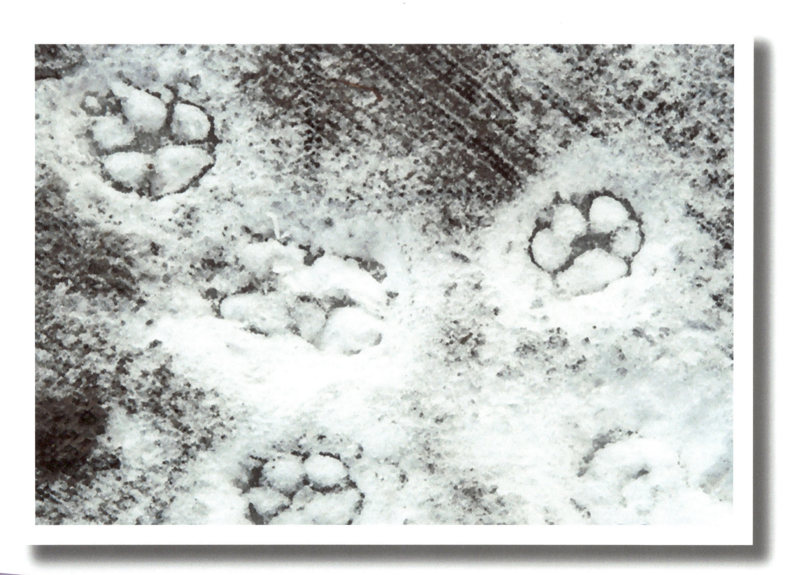

And there she was, oh my, in a drift,
enjoying nature`s abundant winter gift.

I called, here she came
to the open door.
The snow and cold
she wanted no more.

A couch and cuddly pillow found
Tuesday soon was a soft, warm mound.

As Tuesday grew older, knit sweaters kept her warm.
Picking out a new one each day, was the norm.

Tuesday`s friends liked knit items, too,
Especially red, pink and blue.

Some of her sweaters got old and baggy with stains and holes and somewhat snaggy.

She was ready, for me, a hole to darn when she would fetch a ball of yarn.

But sometimes things we cannot mend,
I will always remember my dear, best friend.

The End

CPSIA information can be obtained
at www.ICGtesting.com
Printed in the USA
BVHW092217300123
657483BV00014B/355